All About Me

Name ....

Email ....

School ....

Grade ....

Address ....

Room ....

Phone ....

School Year ....

IMPORTANT INFORMATION TO REMEMBER

....
....
....
....
....
....
....
....
....
....
....
....
....
....
....
....
....
....
....
....
....
....

STUDENTS

NAME	PARENT/GUARDIAN	ADDRESS

PHONE/EMAIL	NOTES

Happy Birthday

JULY	AUGUST	SEPTEMBER

OCTOBER	NOVEMBER	DECEMBER

Celebrate

JANUARY

FEBRUARY

MARCH

APRIL

MAY

JUNE

HOLIDAYS &

JULY

4 Independence Day
› Park and Recreation Month

AUGUST

9 Book Lovers Day
› Get Ready for Kindergarten Month

SEPTEMBER

11 Patriot Day
› Labor Day (1st Monday)
› Grandparents' Day (Sunday After Labor Day)
› Hispanic Heritage Month (Sept. 15–Oct. 15)
› Rosh Hashanah (or October)
› Yom Kippur (or October)
› Native American Day (4th Friday)

OCTOBER

24 United Nations Day
31 Halloween
› Columbus Day (2nd Monday)
› Fire Prevention Week (2nd Week)

NOVEMBER

1 National Family Literacy Day
11 Veterans Day
13 World Kindness Day
› Thanksgiving Day (4th Thursday)
› Hanukkah (or December)

DECEMBER

25 Christmas Day
26 Kwanzaa Begins
31 New Year's Eve

SPECIAL DATES

JANUARY

1 New Year's Day

⟩ Martin Luther King, Jr. Day (3rd Monday)

⟩ Chinese New Year (or February)

FEBRUARY

2 Groundhog Day

14 Valentine's Day

⟩ Black History Month

⟩ Presidents' Day (3rd Monday)

MARCH

17 St. Patrick's Day

⟩ Women's History Month

⟩ Easter (or April)

⟩ Passover (or April)

APRIL

1 April Fool's Day

22 Earth Day

⟩ National Poetry Month

MAY

1 May Day

5 Cinco de Mayo

⟩ Asian-Pacific American Heritage Month

⟩ Teacher Appreciation Week (1st Week)

⟩ Mother's Day (2nd Sunday)

⟩ Memorial Day (Last Monday)

JUNE

14 Flag Day

⟩ Pet Appreciation Week (1st Full Week)

⟩ Father's Day (3rd Sunday)

⟩ National Safety Month

WEEKLY SCHEDULE

TIME	MONDAY	TUESDAY	WEDNESDAY	THURSDAY	FRIDAY

THURSDAY	FRIDAY	SATURDAY

Notes

"One child, one teacher, one book, and one pen can change the world."
—Malala Yousafzai

THURSDAY	FRIDAY	SATURDAY

Notes

THURSDAY	FRIDAY	SATURDAY

Notes

"The greatest glory in living lies not in never falling,
but in rising every time we fall." —Nelson Mandela

THURSDAY	FRIDAY	SATURDAY

Notes

Notes

"Our progress as a nation can be no swifter than our progress in education." —John F. Kennedy

THURSDAY	FRIDAY	SATURDAY

Notes

"You can't use up creativity. The more you use,
the more you have." —Maya Angelou

THURSDAY	FRIDAY	SATURDAY

Notes

THURSDAY	FRIDAY	SATURDAY

Notes

"Conquer anger with love, evil with good, meanness with generosity,
and lies with truth." —Gautama Buddha

THURSDAY	FRIDAY	SATURDAY

Notes

THURSDAY	FRIDAY	SATURDAY

Notes

....
....
....
....
....
....
....
....
....
....
....
....
....
....
....
....
....
....
....
....
....
....
....
....
....
....
....
....
....
....
....
....
....
....
....
....
....
....
....
....

Notes

"If you want others to be happy, practice compassion.
If you want to be happy, practice compassion." —Dalai Lama

THURSDAY	FRIDAY	SATURDAY

Notes

"In a competition of love we'll all share in the victory,
no matter who comes first." —Muhammad Ali

THURSDAY	FRIDAY	SATURDAY

Notes

"You are never strong enough that you don't need help."
—Cesar Chavez

Time:	Time:	Time:	Time:
Subject:	Subject:	Subject:	Subject:

Week #

Time:	Time:	Time:
Subject:	Subject:	Subject:

MONDAY

/

TUESDAY

/

WEDNESDAY

/

THURSDAY

/

FRIDAY

/

| Time: | Time: | Time: | Time: |
| Subject: | Subject: | Subject: | Subject: |

Week #

Time:

Subject:

Time:

Subject:

Time:

Subject:

MONDAY

/

TUESDAY

/

WEDNESDAY

/

THURSDAY

/

FRIDAY

/

Time:	Time:	Time:	Time:
Subject:	Subject:	Subject:	Subject:

Week #

Time:	Time:	Time:
Subject:	Subject:	Subject:

MONDAY

TUESDAY

WEDNESDAY

THURSDAY

FRIDAY

Time:	Time:	Time:	Time:
Subject:	Subject:	Subject:	Subject:

Week #

	Time:	Time:	Time:
	Subject:	Subject:	Subject:

MONDAY

/

TUESDAY

/

WEDNESDAY

/

THURSDAY

/

FRIDAY

/

Time:	Time:	Time:	Time:
Subject:	Subject:	Subject:	Subject:

Week #

Time:

Subject:

Time:

Subject:

Time:

Subject:

MONDAY

TUESDAY

WEDNESDAY

THURSDAY

FRIDAY

Time:	Time:	Time:	Time:
Subject:	Subject:	Subject:	Subject:

Week #

Time:	Time:	Time:
Subject:	Subject:	Subject:

MONDAY

/

TUESDAY

/

WEDNESDAY

/

THURSDAY

/

FRIDAY

/

Time:	Time:	Time:	Time:
Subject:	Subject:	Subject:	Subject:

Week #

Time: Subject:	Time: Subject:	Time: Subject:

MONDAY

/

TUESDAY

/

WEDNESDAY

/

THURSDAY

/

FRIDAY

/

Time:	Time:	Time:	Time:
Subject:	Subject:	Subject:	Subject:

Week #

Time:

Subject:

Time:

Subject:

Time:

Subject:

MONDAY

/

TUESDAY

/

WEDNESDAY

/

THURSDAY

/

FRIDAY

/

Time:	Time:	Time:	Time:
Subject:	Subject:	Subject:	Subject:

Week #

Time:	Time:	Time:
Subject:	Subject:	Subject:

MONDAY

/

TUESDAY

/

WEDNESDAY

/

THURSDAY

/

FRIDAY

/

Time:	Time:	Time:	Time:
Subject:	Subject:	Subject:	Subject:

Week #

Time:	Time:	Time:
Subject:	Subject:	Subject:

MONDAY

/

TUESDAY

/

WEDNESDAY

/

THURSDAY

/

FRIDAY

/

Time:	Time:	Time:	Time:
Subject:	Subject:	Subject:	Subject:

Week #

Time:	Time:	Time:
Subject:	Subject:	Subject:

MONDAY

/

TUESDAY

/

WEDNESDAY

/

THURSDAY

/

FRIDAY

/

Time:	Time:	Time:	Time:
Subject:	Subject:	Subject:	Subject:

Week #

Time:	Time:	Time:
Subject:	Subject:	Subject:

MONDAY

/

TUESDAY

/

WEDNESDAY

/

THURSDAY

/

FRIDAY

/

Time:	Time:	Time:	Time:
Subject:	Subject:	Subject:	Subject:

Week #

Time:

Subject:

Time:

Subject:

Time:

Subject:

MONDAY

TUESDAY

WEDNESDAY

THURSDAY

FRIDAY

| Time: | Time: | Time: | Time: |
| Subject: | Subject: | Subject: | Subject: |

Week #

Time:	Time:	Time:
Subject:	Subject:	Subject:

MONDAY

/

TUESDAY

/

WEDNESDAY

/

THURSDAY

/

FRIDAY

/

Time:

Subject:

Time:

Subject:

Time:

Subject:

Time:

Subject:

Week #

Time: Subject:	Time: Subject:	Time: Subject:

MONDAY

/

TUESDAY

/

WEDNESDAY

/

THURSDAY

/

FRIDAY

/

Time:	Time:	Time:	Time:
Subject:	Subject:	Subject:	Subject:

Week #

Time: _____
Subject: _____

Time: _____
Subject: _____

Time: _____
Subject: _____

MONDAY

/

TUESDAY

/

WEDNESDAY

/

THURSDAY

/

FRIDAY

/

Time:	Time:	Time:	Time:
Subject:	Subject:	Subject:	Subject:

Week #

Time: Subject:	Time: Subject:	Time: Subject:

MONDAY

/

TUESDAY

/

WEDNESDAY

/

THURSDAY

/

FRIDAY

/

Time:

Subject:

Time:

Subject:

Time:

Subject:

Time:

Subject:

Week #

Time: | Time: | Time:
Subject: | Subject: | Subject:

MONDAY

/

TUESDAY

/

WEDNESDAY

/

THURSDAY

/

FRIDAY

/

Time:	Time:	Time:	Time:
Subject:	Subject:	Subject:	Subject:

Week #

MONDAY

/

TUESDAY

/

WEDNESDAY

/

THURSDAY

/

FRIDAY

/

Time:

Subject:

Time:

Subject:

Time:

Subject:

Time:	Time:	Time:	Time:
Subject:	Subject:	Subject:	Subject:

Week #

Time:	Time:	Time:
Subject:	Subject:	Subject:

MONDAY

/

TUESDAY

/

WEDNESDAY

/

THURSDAY

/

FRIDAY

/

Time:	Time:	Time:	Time:
Subject:	Subject:	Subject:	Subject:

Week #

Time:	Time:	Time:
Subject:	Subject:	Subject:

MONDAY

/

TUESDAY

/

WEDNESDAY

/

THURSDAY

/

FRIDAY

/

Time:	Time:	Time:	Time:
Subject:	Subject:	Subject:	Subject:

....
....
....
....
....
....

....
....
....
....
....

....
....
....
....
....
....

....
....
....
....
....
....

....
....
....
....
....

Week #

Time:	Time:	Time:
Subject:	Subject:	Subject:

MONDAY

/

TUESDAY

/

WEDNESDAY

/

THURSDAY

/

FRIDAY

/

Time:	Time:	Time:	Time:
Subject:	Subject:	Subject:	Subject:

Week #

Time:	Time:	Time:
Subject:	Subject:	Subject:

MONDAY

/

TUESDAY

/

WEDNESDAY

/

THURSDAY

/

FRIDAY

/

Time:	Time:	Time:	Time:
Subject:	Subject:	Subject:	Subject:

Week #

Time:

Subject:

Time:

Subject:

Time:

Subject:

MONDAY

/

TUESDAY

/

WEDNESDAY

/

THURSDAY

/

FRIDAY

/

Time:	Time:	Time:	Time:
Subject:	Subject:	Subject:	Subject:

Week #

Time:	Time:	Time:
Subject:	Subject:	Subject:

MONDAY

/

TUESDAY

/

WEDNESDAY

/

THURSDAY

/

FRIDAY

/

Time:	Time:	Time:	Time:
Subject:	Subject:	Subject:	Subject:

Week #

Time:	Time:	Time:
Subject:	Subject:	Subject:

MONDAY

/

TUESDAY

/

WEDNESDAY

/

THURSDAY

/

FRIDAY

/

Time:	Time:	Time:	Time:
Subject:	Subject:	Subject:	Subject:

Week #

Time:	Time:	Time:
Subject:	Subject:	Subject:

MONDAY

/

TUESDAY

/

WEDNESDAY

/

THURSDAY

/

FRIDAY

/

Time:	Time:	Time:	Time:
Subject:	Subject:	Subject:	Subject:

....
....
....
....
....
....

....
....
....
....
....
....

....
....
....
....
....
....

....
....
....
....
....
....

....
....
....
....
....

Week #

Time:	Time:	Time:
Subject:	Subject:	Subject:

MONDAY

/

TUESDAY

/

WEDNESDAY

/

THURSDAY

/

FRIDAY

/

Time:

Subject:

Time:

Subject:

Time:

Subject:

Time:

Subject:

Week #

Time:	Time:	Time:
Subject:	Subject:	Subject:

MONDAY

/

TUESDAY

/

WEDNESDAY

/

THURSDAY

/

FRIDAY

/

Time:	Time:	Time:	Time:
Subject:	Subject:	Subject:	Subject:

....

....

....

....

....

....

....

....

....

....

....

....

....

....

....

....

....

....

....

....

....

....

....

....

Week #

Time:	Time:	Time:
Subject:	Subject:	Subject:

MONDAY

/

TUESDAY

/

WEDNESDAY

/

THURSDAY

/

FRIDAY

/

Time:	Time:	Time:	Time:
Subject:	Subject:	Subject:	Subject:

Week #

Time:

Subject:

Time:

Subject:

Time:

Subject:

MONDAY

/

TUESDAY

/

WEDNESDAY

/

THURSDAY

/

FRIDAY

/

Time:	Time:	Time:	Time:
Subject:	Subject:	Subject:	Subject:

Week #

| Time: | Time: | Time: |
| Subject: | Subject: | Subject: |

MONDAY

/

TUESDAY

/

WEDNESDAY

/

THURSDAY

/

FRIDAY

/

Time:	Time:	Time:	Time:
Subject:	Subject:	Subject:	Subject:

Week #

Time:	Time:	Time:
Subject:	Subject:	Subject:

MONDAY

/

TUESDAY

/

WEDNESDAY

/

THURSDAY

/

FRIDAY

/

Time:	Time:	Time:	Time:
Subject:	Subject:	Subject:	Subject:

Week #

Time:	Time:	Time:
Subject:	Subject:	Subject:

MONDAY

/

TUESDAY

/

WEDNESDAY

/

THURSDAY

/

FRIDAY

/

Time:	Time:	Time:	Time:
Subject:	Subject:	Subject:	Subject:

Week #

| Time: | Time: | Time: |
| Subject: | Subject: | Subject: |

MONDAY

/

TUESDAY

/

WEDNESDAY

/

THURSDAY

/

FRIDAY

/

Time:

Subject:

Time:

Subject:

Time:

Subject:

Time:

Subject:

Week #

Time:

Subject:

Time:

Subject:

Time:

Subject:

MONDAY

/

TUESDAY

/

WEDNESDAY

/

THURSDAY

/

FRIDAY

/

Time:	Time:	Time:	Time:
Subject:	Subject:	Subject:	Subject:

Week #

Time:

Subject:

Time:

Subject:

Time:

Subject:

MONDAY

/

TUESDAY

/

WEDNESDAY

/

THURSDAY

/

FRIDAY

/

| Time: | Time: | Time: | Time: |
| Subject: | Subject: | Subject: | Subject: |

....
....
....
....
....
....

....
....
....
....
....

....
....
....
....
....

....
....
....
....
....

....
....
....
....
....

Week #

Time: \
Subject:

Time: \
Subject:

Time: \
Subject:

MONDAY

/

TUESDAY

/

WEDNESDAY

/

THURSDAY

/

FRIDAY

/

Time:	Time:	Time:	Time:
Subject:	Subject:	Subject:	Subject:

Week #

Time:

Subject:

Time:

Subject:

Time:

Subject:

MONDAY

/

TUESDAY

/

WEDNESDAY

/

THURSDAY

/

FRIDAY

/

Time:

Subject:

Time:

Subject:

Time:

Subject:

Time:

Subject:

Week #

Time:	Time:	Time:
Subject:	Subject:	Subject:

MONDAY

/

TUESDAY

/

WEDNESDAY

/

THURSDAY

/

FRIDAY

/

Time:	Time:	Time:	Time:
Subject:	Subject:	Subject:	Subject:

Notes

Design by Mina Chen. Illustrations by Anni Betts.